Practical Politics for Local Agency Board Members

Practical Politics for Local Agency Board Members

David C. Antonucci

Table of Contents

Introduction

Practical politics is about being active and getting things done in the public policy arena. As all levels of government continue to redefine roles and responsibilities and experience funding cuts, the task of making government more effective becomes extremely difficult. Add to this difficulty the paradox of the public wanting less government intrusion while simultaneously demanding more government services and problem-solving actions. All this serves to make political effectiveness more important but much more difficult to achieve,

> **Practical Politics is what you do to increase personal effectiveness and achieve political success.**

The author's goal is to package his 33-plus years of public sector experience into a useful guide on the elements of practical politics for elected officials. This is not a theoretical work for policy wonks; instead, it is a compendium of practicalities needed to achieve political success in a challenging environment. Think of this as a field manual on effectiveness in the political arena.

Knowledge is experience applied to information. Information comes in a myriad of ways: direct experience, learned facts and published works of others. This book is no different; it relies on all these sources, and several deserve special credit. Some of the concepts developed in this book came from Richard Haas's <u>Power to Persuade</u> and various books on political relationships and negotiations by Roger Fisher and Robert Ury. You will also discover influences from many others throughout the text and find them cataloged in the suggested reading list.

The author would like to acknowledge the support of his life partner and spouse, Jennifer Antonucci. Good friends Jack Sanchez and Ed Miller edited and reviewed the manuscript.

Read and learn from this book; then make it happen!

David C. Antonucci
Tahoma, CA

Understanding Political Context

Local government is a creation of the state as the means for delivering governmental services at the local level. Included in this category are cities, towns, counties and special districts.

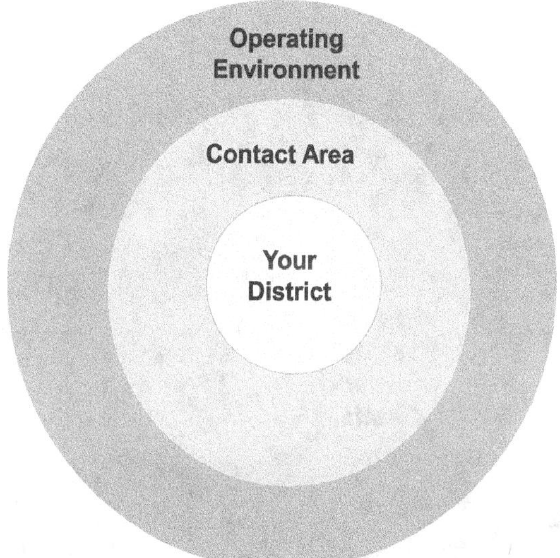

Think of a local government model as concentric rings. In the center ring is the agency itself. In the outer ring is the general operating environment that affects the agency. The

middle ring represents the contact area where the public services produced by the agency become confluent with the external operating environment. This model can be adapted to various forms of local government.

The next diagram shows the local government model fully fleshed out with the specific characteristics of each ring shown.

In the center, the area is the four main resources available to local government. People in the form of board and staff carry out the mission of the agency. Infrastructure is the totality of all physical assets available to produce public services and

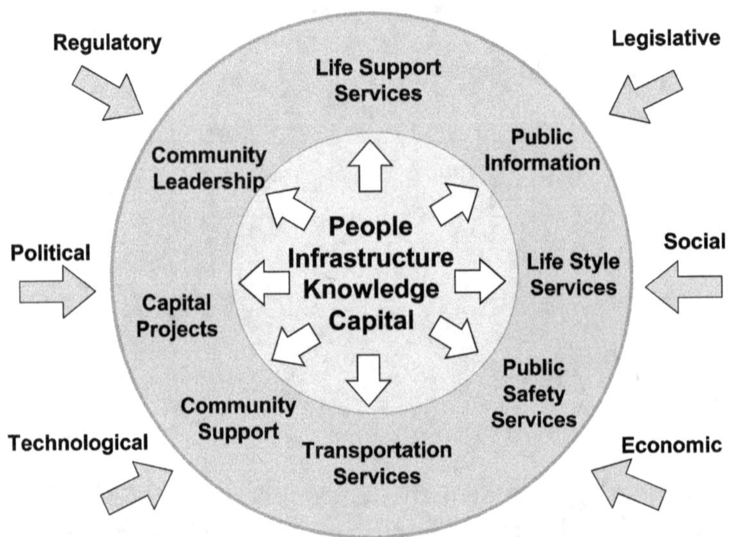

includes equipment and public works. Capital is the financial wherewithal to fund the ongoing production of services and includes such financial assets as grants, fees, taxes, and reserves. Knowledge and exper-

Knowledge is the overarching resource that allows utilization of all other resources efficiently and effectively.

tise are intangible, but nonetheless valuable resources that accumulate over time much like a monetary investment. Knowledge is the overarching resource that allows utilization of all other resources to produce efficient and effective government services.

The middle ring is where public services meet the external operating environment. Aside from the standard tangible services that customers can see, touch or experience, there are intangible services that are a natural product of governmental activity. Some examples are preparing leaders for higher office, overall community guidance and problem-solving and public information on issues unrelated to the agency's mission.

In the operating environment ring, outside forces exert influence on the public services and the agency itself. These forces represent a broad range of external powers that can arise from local, regional, statewide, national and even international effects. Understand that the external operating environment functions independently and somewhat randomly. This is the key to knowing an agency and these forces will dynamically affect its service products. Further, these forces often have a rippling effect all the way back into the internal ring of available resources.

The Political Terrain

Much like mountains, rivers and valleys characterize physical terrain, agencies, special interest groups, and community members, amid many, create "political" ground. Just as steep mountains can be treacherous, entrenched special interest groups can create similar danger. Fully understanding the operating environment invites the metaphorical use of a compass and map to navigate to political success. Positioning and navigation skills become the metaphor for Practical Politics. This diagram illustrates a typical political terrain map for local government.

Political Navigation

If we use terrain as the metaphor for political environment, then the compass becomes the instrument of choice to metaphorically locate, map and navigate a path to political success. To begin, imagine that the cardinal points of the compass indicate the direction to a specific political terrain feature. To the North are the persons/entities that exert authority. To the South are persons/entities subject to sovereignty. In the East lie those who have equal power of partnership. Westward are those who are influential or subject to influence. Finally, the center of the compass rose marks one's position on the map of the political terrain.

8

Agency Positioning

As one can imagine, the position of a local government agency is quite complex with nearly countless factors in its operating environment. In the Authority position of the North reside the judicial, legislative, regulatory regional government forces together with the local electorate. Since the electorate casts the only votes in a democratic election, it has absolute power, compared to the broader community or even special interests. Westward in the Partnership direction are joint powers agencies, neighboring local governments and granting agencies, all of whom have comparable power to the agency itself. To the East in the Influence location lie broad and variable influences such as community, lesser local governments, and influential special interests. Looking South in the direction of Sovereignty, beyond are the precious few interests in which a local government has some control, such as users, customers, employee organizations and private contractors.

In a dynamic operating environment, each of these organizations and loosely formed communities of interest can experience ebb and flow of power, causing them to rotate into different positions around the compass rose. Such factors as
controversial issues, infusion of resources and affiliation with
a powerful ally can affect their location on the political terrain
map.

Board Member Positioning

Referring again to the compass metaphor, a local agency
board member can find a myriad of political factors and influences at the four points of the compass. At the top
Authority position, are the public, community, and electorate.
In the Partnership location are peer board members. Inhabit-
ing the Influence compass point are the many that have a
keen interest in the agency, but who lack comparable power
such as various incarnations of local and state government

along with organized pressure groups. The sole confidential employee of any board member or board of directors occupies the slot below Sovereignty; that is, the chief executive

officer, i.e., general manager or fire chief. The board exerts almost absolute authority over this incumbent, except for ethics. Ethical allegiance is to the public, not the board.

In the following sections, this text will more carefully examine the board member compass points and plot a path to political effectiveness.

Center of the Compass: The Board Member

The center of the compass marks position, in effect identifying the location and the direction to the cardinal compass points. The board member is at the compass center, a point at which the individual looks outward in all directions. At the very center are the essential characteristics one must practice to be effective.

See the Big Picture

A crucial characteristic is to be able to see the "Big Picture" in the form of broader issues, recurring themes, overarching trends and the passage of time. However, the Big Picture is not a vision. Seeing the Big Picture allows one to pull away from details and minutiae, advancing directly to the most effective solution, key issue or underlying motivator. In essence, seeing the Big Picture is a disciplined thinking process that determines what constitutes reality, discards the irrelevant facts, places remaining facts in context, extracts conclusions and produces real knowledge. This is already a challenging skill to acquire, and few can master it.

Have an Open Agenda and Follow It

Effective board members have an agenda and stick to it. An opportunistic candidate ran an extremely negative campaign, continually criticizing the local government agency. Once elected, he attended an issues workshop but sat silently through two days of discussions. The apparent problem was that he had nothing to say because he had never given any thought to what he would do if elected. He had revealed himself as an ineffective and intellectually weak public official.

Competent public officials know what they want and have a plan to get it.

Competent public officials know what they want and have a plan to get it. They make others aware of it and keep their intentions

12

transparent. This methodology is the heart of forming an open agenda.

Developing an agenda is challenging but straightforward. Brainstorm problems and solutions to arrive at a very long list of potential actions. Reduce the list by consolidating and tossing duplicative actions. Prioritize the resulting list based on importance and feasibility. Select 3-5 actions from the top tier to form the agenda, then execute. Recognize that most of the government advances by increment and rarely by a significant paradigm shift. For this reason, agenda items should be objectives that are just beyond grasp, requiring a stretch rather than a jump to achieve. Repeat this process yearly or as factors change.

Act with Competence and Credibility

Credibility and its product, effectiveness, come from consistently acting with demonstrable competence. Organized data produces Information. Knowledge is an interpretation of information. Experience is the lens through which one views knowledge, adding nuances of interpretation, exceptions and past successes. Acting with knowledge and experience yields competence. Gathering intelligence and experience in three key areas is necessary.

Board members must be well versed in general background information, agency information and issue-specific information. Background information covers enabling legislation and related laws, conflicts of interest and open meetings. Awareness of current governmental issues will nicely round out background comprehension. Association sponsored training sessions for board members to provide these basics

and are mandatory for establishing knowledge and competence.

Standard agency information is composed of infrastructure
inventory, master plans, policies and procedures, and ordi-
nances. Add to these the agency history and the nature of the
organizational culture as supplemental references.

Researching and verifying all relevant facts, viewpoints, op-
tions, and consequences will yield the issue-specific information needed.

A competent action comes from a complete knowledge base
and broad experience. Knowing that the words and actions
of public officials are constantly being scrutinized demands
that you always speak and act with competence.

Build Trust into Words and Actions

Trust is a massive structure built over time. The Egyptians constructed great pyramids over decades with materials made to stand through the ages. Similarly, the individual builds trust pyramid style over time from the content of a solid character.

Trust

Open Agenda

Share Information

Honesty & Integrity

Predictable Behavior

Consult Before Deciding

Respect Confidentiality & Loyalty

Keep Promises & Honor Commitments

The first course of blocks are the simple principles of making an individual's actions conform to their commitments and thus avoid a career-crippling reputation being labeled as "unreliable." The next course of block work is showing others that one can be entrusted with sensitive information and remain loyal to others who are absent. Higher up one lays out a path of consulting with affected parties before deciding. Consistent, predictable behavior reassures others, builds a sense of safety and situation control and accommodates joint risk-taking by others. Honesty is a simple concept -- ensuring that one's communications conform to reality and are accurate and complete. Integrity is validating one's words with corresponding actions. Sharing information reinforces openness and fairness in interpersonal relations. An open agenda shows others that an individual's intentions and motives are clear. The capstone is an aura of trust that accompanies a person throughout their career.

Public Trust and Public Interest Control

The public trust and public interest are not the same. The public trust principle means that the public expects one will never act in one's own self-interest in one's role as a democratic representative. Conflict of interest rules come into play here and are the direct result of abuses of the public trust.

You must always incorporate the public trust and public interest into your actions.

Public interest dictates that a public official's actions shall be for the greatest benefit for the broadest community of interest. However, this does not mean that the public interest requires equal benefits for all. Applying the public interest means one acts ethically for the benefit of the many but protects the rights of the few.

When acting in the fiduciary role as a public official one must always incorporate the public trust and the public interest into their words and actions. Always understand that these principles control. There are no permissible exceptions, rationalizations or circumventions. Likewise, there are no excuses for ignoring the public interest.

North: Authority: Political Direction

The current reality is that the notion of democracy has been changing from representative democracy to a participatory democracy model. The republican democracy model conceives people advancing to public office through a democratic process and representing the will of the people.

Representatives are not delegates; they are free to vote their conscience while considering the public view. They only become accountable during an election. Participatory democracy envisions a direct democracy where the will of the people always prevails. Representatives are becoming more constrained as voters diminish or rescind their legislative powers and transfer more control to the people. Yet the paradoxical reality is that people do not want to be bothered with the policy decisions that public officials must make in their role as democratic representatives. The reasonable approach is to retain representative government while ensuring the highest level of opportunity for public involvement.

Determining the Public View

The public view is like the tide – high then low; waning then waxing; at times comforting like an ebb tide; then treacherous like a riptide or toxic like a red tide. Like tide monitoring and prediction, public officials must continuously measure and predict the public view. The science of public opinion polling has created a whole industry. Fortunately, local public officials have less intensive, but nonetheless effective, techniques to gauge the depths of the public view.

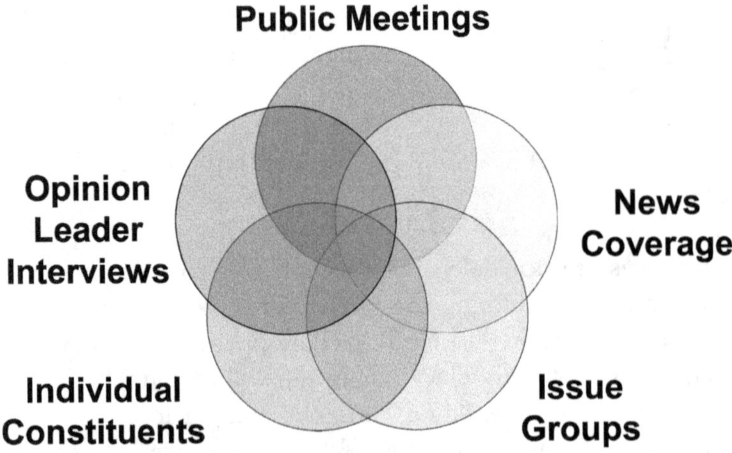

An astute public official can take advantage of readily available sources of information. When assessing the public view, keep in mind no one source is of itself conclusive. Scan all sources for areas of commonality and overlapping themes of public concern as illustrated in the diagram.

Public officials must continuously monitor and gauge the public view.

Public meetings in which citizens may be speaking out on any issue are fruitful places to gather public opinion. At public meetings, citizens will not only speak to the topic but will reveal their attitudes toward governance. News coverage is another source since media interviews and quotes citizens on a variety of community issues. Scheduling a listening and feedback session with opinion leaders can be very productive. One should target these sessions at other public officials, business leaders, citizen activists and service club members. In small towns, barbers, hairdressers, and bartenders are valuable sources that have a good understanding of the public view!

The listen-feedback technique applies to "average citizens." Ask open-ended questions, listen and then respond by repeating what the listener heard. Any citizen is flattered that his or her own opinion matters.

Consider using informally organized issue groups. These are not focus groups. Issue groups can be broadly composed or selected according to interest in a specific issue. Use the same open-ended, probing technique, write down comments on a flip chart, do not directly challenge statements and do not seek to get a consensus. Observe the interaction among group members and the reactions to statements made by other group members.

Of course, the public forums and public comment on agenda items for the agency is yet another good source. The key points to accurately determining the public view are a diversity of sources, continuous collection of information and periodic recalibration of the public opinion.

Be Visible and Accessible

Be where the public is. Attend community social functions, volunteer for community projects, visit service clubs and attend local sporting events to increase visibility. People may not like a public official, but they love seeing high visibility people! Accessibility is a problem for public officials, particularly those with a well-known public persona. Perceived stature and their own feelings of self-confidence sometimes intimidate people. Be accessible by being approachable. Initiate eye contact, offer to introduce yourself and project friendliness. Board members can publish their home phone number, email address and encourage their use as a communication channel.

Show Respect and Concern

Many members of the public are grossly suspicious and distrustful of public officials. They actively look for evidence to reinforce this belief. If board members do not show respect and concern when dealing with the public, they just play into the hands of critics. Following a few simple principles will dispel any notions among the people that an official is not receptive or even interested in their concerns.

- Allow the public to express their feelings fully without interruption and within a reasonable amount of allotted time.
- Ask follow-up questions to explain and clarify their statements.

- Record the substance of the comment on a flip chart or have the presiding officer verbally summarize what the comments.
- Diplomatically challenge patently untruthful, defamatory or inflammatory statements.

At times, the public will aim its criticism directly at an individual board member, whether they are responsible or not. Responding to direct criticism requires special handling and careful diplomacy. Follow these steps:

- Assess the comments – Evaluate substance, credibility, context, and importance. Respond only if relevant. If the critic is right, make an acknowledgment and declare the matter closed.
- Seek to understand – Acknowledge the criticism and ask specific questions for clarification.
- Disarm the critic – Find some aspect of the critic or criticism that is agreeable, but do not validate the entire critique.
- Defend oneself – Tactfully and assertively explain the situation from another point of view while acknowledging the possible validity of other points of view
- Conclude the exchange – Try to bring closure by agreement of what is fact or committing to follow-up action.

Shape Public Opinion

Like it or not, as a public official, you are automatically viewed as a community opinion leader. As such, community members look to an official for answers and will weight those views heavily. Seize the opportunity! Board members can effectively shape public opinion. Do not be deterred by extreme individualists and others who openly reject authority figures. They constitute a tiny segment, though they probably receive more attention than they deserve.

The official's own words are the most potent tool to influence public opinion. An official can easily make a brief impromptu speech on any familiar topic by following this simple formula for leaders. First, state what constitutes reality by separating fact from fiction and filtering out the irrelevant. Next, describe the context of these facts by adding meaning through an explanation of how these affect the constituency. Finally, construct a word picture of how things may play out. If unsure, use several potential scenarios. Be sure to mix in personal opinion of how things should be. Remember: separate fact, explain the context and depict the future.

A simple impromptu speech formula is facts, context and future scenario.

West: Partnership: Peer Board Members

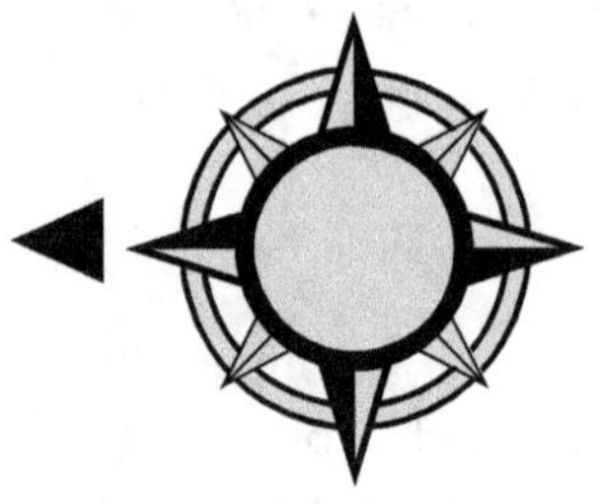

Your peer board members are equals and partners. All share the same power, authority, and status. Yet, none has power, authority or status unless they function as a partnership. The power comes from the group, with no one person having the ability to enact policy unilaterally. Political effectiveness is mainly dependent on interaction with partners and the quality of the relationships.

Maintain Communication and Relationship

The goal of any political liaison is positive outcomes that benefit the agency and creation of a constructive ongoing relationship. In a situation where there is no apparent authority over others, a public official should employ techniques to achieve persuasive leadership. If position power is merely unavailable; one must exercise any accumulated personal power derived from credibility, trustworthiness, and competence. Aside from personal power, compelling leadership also relies on a sense of common interests, interpersonal connectedness, influence, inclusion, and participatory decision-making.

An individual can build on commonality by emphasizing similar views, beliefs and values, comparable personal agenda and a calling to public service to form a relationship with peer board members. Downplay differences and accept them as good for diversity. Reframe discrepancies as an alternate approach based on shared values.

Personal power comes from credibility and trustworthiness.

Create interpersonal connectedness by expressing support whenever possible. Embrace another's problem and solve it together. Seek input from others and respond positively. Express sincere appreciation and lavishly dole out credit.

Use persuasion over coercion. Use logical arguments and appeal to the shared values of others. Show the similarities with their approach. Refrain from coercive threats or political "payback."

Make sure all discussions are inclusive. Do not exclude dissenters unless they are verbally abusive or highly disruptive. Make sure to follow applicable open meeting laws and avoid "sidebar" conversations at board meetings.

Function as a Board

By far, the most common board member dysfunction is trying to act independently. Attempting to circumvent the full board by unilaterally pressuring staff leads to disorganization and crossed purposes.

The agency enabling legislation almost certainly sought to achieve balance in governance. Enabling acts mandate diversity by authorizing a multi-person governing body over one individual as governor. The board serves the dual function of the elected legislative branch and elected executive branch in local government. One exception is a separately elected mayor in a strong mayor-council form of city government.

The best boards function as a team.

The clear legislative intent is to broaden governance while not allowing any one person to have unilateral power. The board must act as a whole for an action to be valid. Policy issues must come through the full council for approval. Some boards delegate the authority for policy formulation to board committees, but a majority of board members must still make the final decision. Some boards may require a board review of non-policy items such as board member information requests.

Until the governing body can learn to function as a whole, agency efficiency and effectiveness will suffer. The best boards work like a team with each member sticking to the batting order and playing their assigned positions.

Engage All Members and Seek Consensus

An essential job of the presiding officer is to be sure that all members fully engage, and the board decision process is oriented toward consensus. Full engagement ensures that all points of view be heard and considered. Consensus oriented decision processes seek compromise, additions, and deletions to proposed actions so that everyone can vote in the affirmative, if possible.

Engagement and consensus building is a cyclical process that must be repeated to achieve its full effect. Cycling through the steps is mostly the responsibility of the presiding officer

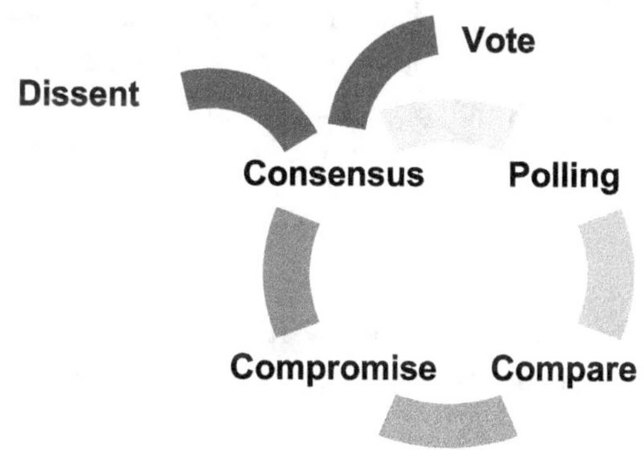

with board member support. Consensus does not mean una-
nimity and further allows that disagreement is permissible if
reasonable attempts fail to produce an agreement.

Once a motion on a disputed issue receives a second, but before discussion concludes, the presiding officer should call on
or "poll" each board member to express his or her position
on the motion. Once all members have spoken, the group
compares the views and identifies any fundamental differences. Any member can suggest modifications to the proposed action in an attempt to achieve a consensus and deci-
sive vote. If this initial attempt is unsuccessful, the cycle
should repeat. If after several cycles, it is apparent no further
progress is possible, the board should acknowledge the dis-
sent and proceed to vote on the measure. As an act of
acknowledgment, the presiding officer should note for the
record that one or more board members dissented for stated
reasons.

A board member should honor and respect the final decision of the board.

Being on the losing end of a crucial vote is not pleasant and can be quite humiliating. No matter how strongly the dissenting board member feels, the board member should respect and honor the board's decision. This acceptance means the debate is over and now the opposition should cooperate with the majority wishes.

Dissenters should refrain from undermining the decision, publicly criticizing the rest of the board members or using unethical means to overturn the decision. They are not required to help, but neither should they be obstructionists. Prevailing board members should reciprocate with graciousness toward the dissenters and reinforce their desire to continue working together for the public good.

South: Sovereignty: Subordinates

The southern cardinal compass point represents those over which the board exerts sovereignty. In a practical sense, this  means those who work for you, specifically, the chief executive officer or the chief administrative officer. A CEO has delegated authority to render judgment in the execution and interpretation of policy orders of the board. The Chief Administrative Officer has no power to exercise discretion, only the ability to execute policy orders as prescribed. The CAO must return to the governing board for interpretation and exceptions. The CAO situation is symptomatic of board micromanagement.

Define the Relationship by the Expectations

Specifying the formal relationship between the board and its CEO requires both parties to define and agree on their mutual expectations. Four key areas determine the nature of each party's expectations: delegation of authority, results, resource allocation, and controls.

A delegation of the authority is crucial to effective functioning and specificity, essential for delegation. The delegation
agreement is the foundation of Board-management relations.
This document lays out the amount of authority, expected
results, controls, and reporting, and allocation of resources,
all for the purpose of execution of board policy directives.
Perhaps the best way to delegate authority is to transfer all
power necessary to run the agency with the board retaining
defined specific jurisdiction. Specific and quantitative descrip-
tion of results is best. These are usually composed of the
appropriate level of service standards and yearly goals and
objectives. Controls and reporting further refine the boundaries of authority by defining which actions to carry out unilaterally, actions to report to the board before execution and
actions to report to the board after the fact. An annual budget ideally encapsulates the financial and personnel resource
allocations. A good budget document contains these essential
elements:

- Expense allocations by category – personnel, charges
  and services, materials and supplies, and administration
- Level of service standards

- Performance indicators
- Personnel allocation
- Capital project spending

Evaluation of Performance

Board members are often uncomfortable with a performance evaluation of the CEO. Unstructured evaluation sessions are awkward and at times can become acrimonious, doing damage to all participants. Far too many are just not done or just swept under the rug. Usually, these afflictions are the result of untrained board members being unable to do useful performance evaluations.

There is a better way that is simple and straightforward. First, make sure all aspects of the board-manager relationship are solidified and reducing to writing. Select a standard executive evaluation form and have all parties review it together. This will be the annual evaluation instrument. During the year, conduct brief feedback sessions with the CEO in a private setting and record the content.

Before the annual evaluation, distribute the evaluation instrument to all board members and the CEO. Concurrently, the CEO should prepare a report on results achieved, compared to expected results.

The presiding officer or a board committee collect each board member's completed evaluation instrument and obtains the verbal comments from each. The presiding officer or committee tabulates the results and organizes verbal feedback. Carefully review this document the CEO together with the CEO's report on results. The presiding officer, the committee or the board as a whole can do this. Optionally, the CEO completes a self-evaluation and presents it at this meeting. The full body should vote on the final evaluation with results submitted to the CEO's personnel file.

Advice, Consultation and Micromanagement

Board members should always feel free to offer clear advice or seek consultation with the CEO on matters of concern. Frequently, board members have expertise in technical areas such as finance, engineering, public relations, construction, and law. They can be useful resources, especially in a small district. However, never allow offering advice or seeking consultation to degenerate into micromanagement.

Micromanagement is a widespread affliction in public agencies. Enabling legislation for local agencies has no restrictions on what activities board members may engage in as part of their fiduciary duty. Technically, a board can directly manage employees, and many small agencies do just that out of necessity. However, all district, city and county associations strongly discourage this practice.

Micromanagement occurs when a board thinks they know better than management and takes direct control of an issue. Admittedly, this type of action is demoralizing as well as inefficient and very risky. The most popular areas of micromanagement are personnel issues, vehicle selection, the award of professional service contracts and customer service problems. Some legal experts believe a board member acquires personal liability for his/her micromanagement actions if the acts are outside the scope of board policy.

If micromanagement is present and accompanied by mutual distrust, then both management and the board need to revisit the delegation agreement. Micromanagement is a slippery slope; take a step, and suddenly the board is all the way in and up to its neck in the quicksand of mismanagement and confusion.

East: Influence: External Organizations

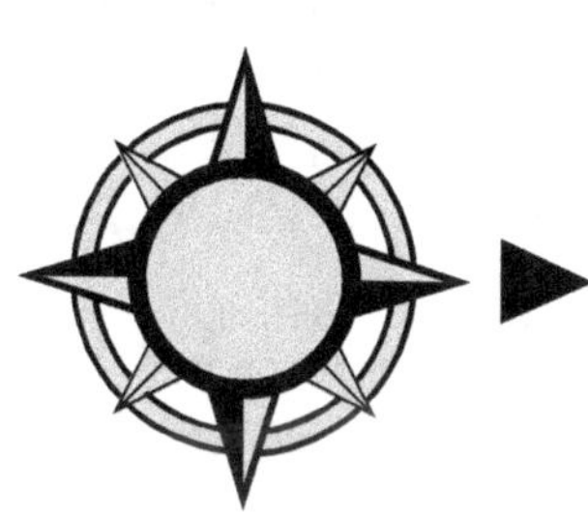

To the east are forces that will attempt to exert influence on the board. In response, the board should direct its weight at these parties. These forces are primarily composed of organizations and prominent individuals. One cannot control them, nor can they manage the board. However, both sides would like to exert influence over the other. Consider these steps to build strong two-way bridges to external organizations.

Establish Relationships with Key Leaders

The board members and CEO of external organizations are the leading prospects for establishing political relations. Creating an ongoing, productive working relationship takes work, but pays handsome dividends. An effective political relationship creates the incentive for others to collaborate to preserve a relationship they value. Political connections require patience and dili-

Political relationships require patience and diligence.

gence to maintain viability, but they yield beneficial results and stable relations. Adopt the philosophy of acting unconditionally constructive, doing what is good for the agency and the relationship, even if others do not reciprocate.

Implement these suggested strategies to improve your external working relationships.

- Seek to understand the other position before stating your opinion. Start by grasping the group's organizational mission and its role in the political arena.
- Use persuasive arguments over coercive tactics. Coercion may get results one time, but it forever poisons the future.
- Practice frequent communication and contact while providing continuous information to them. Keep the lines open and functioning.
- Create an environment of trust by acting trustworthy. Refer to the elements of trustworthiness in Center of the Compass.
- Substitute reason for emotion. If the other party acts with passion, acknowledge the feelings but do not respond in kind.
- Accept them "as is." Do not condemn or criticize their behavior.
- Continue implementing these strategies even if they do not reciprocate, but not if they attack or strongly oppose your agency.

Know Local Legislators
Local governments are creations of the state to provide for local delivery of public services. Naturally, the legislature will

want to continuously dabble in local agency affairs and saddle it with unrealistic demands. This interference from above is why knowing local legislators are a critical component of political effectiveness.

Legislators are persons who have VIP status and want ceremonial treatment. Start by visiting them in their state and federal offices. Attend their fundraisers and support them publicly. Provide them with facility tours and dinner meetings with the board. Every time you meet, have single page unbiased summaries of current issues accompanied by the agency positions. Write letters and make phone calls to influence their legislative activities. Provide them with useful background information and early alerts about developing community issues. In summary, be helpful, be available and stay in touch.

Chart the Course

The board member can now put navigation skills to use by plotting a course through political terrain to political effectiveness. Readers may photocopy for personal use only the compass rose template at the end of this book to serve as a base map. At each cardinal point, brainstorm the many political landmarks occurring at that point.

First consolidate, then prioritize the landmarks with the highest being those landmarks that have the most impact or the most potential to be influenced. Redraw your terrain map with these highest priority landmarks plotted.

Review the navigational strategies associated with each of the four cardinal points and connect these to the particular landmark on the terrain map. Navigate to each marker and increased political effectiveness.

Should one get lost, use these five stationary beacons of absolute reference points to reestablish position:

- Build trust in every statement and action.
- Define expectations with others.
- Engage peers.
- Keep abreast of the public view.
- Invoke the principles of sound political relations.

Phases of Board Development

Boards have very distinct phases of development in the process of moving toward productivity and effectiveness. Most importantly as a presiding officer, and secondarily as a board

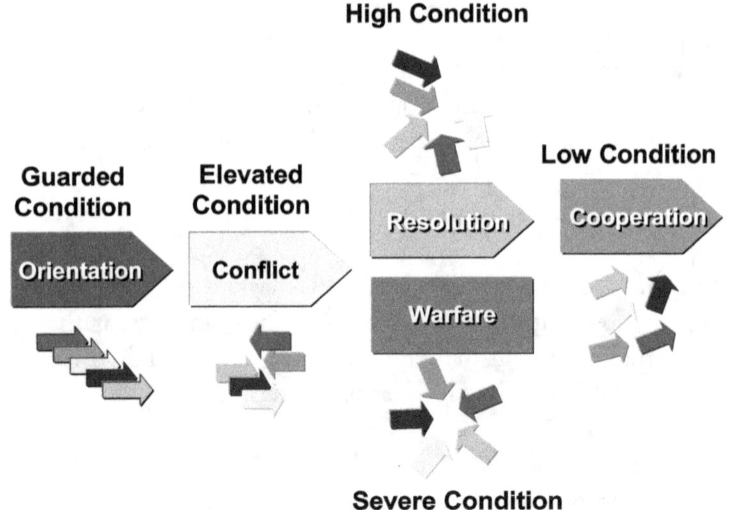

member, one must be able to diagnose the current phase and apply the principles of situational leadership. Situational leadership is the process of adapting your leadership style to two key indicators that describe the followers.

These key indicators are the competence level of individuals and the group as a whole, and the nature of the relationship among the group members. Where these indicators fall on the measurement spectra will determine leadership style. In subsequent sections, examination of each phase occurs in more detail along with recommended situational leadership styles.

This process diagram shows the phases and their sequence. The smaller arrows schematically represent the board members of a five-person board and their alignment at each step. It seems appropriate to adopt the Department of Homeland Security alertness scale to describe the general atmosphere at each stage.

Keep in mind a board may cycle through these phases at any time, including regression to previous phases. Any significant change in personnel, alteration of power dynamics or the emergence of controversial issues could precipitate phase movement. In any event, boards will start phasing every two years if for no other reason than the anxiety of a pending election. Addition of new members or loss of existing board members will always trigger phase change episodes until the board once again attains stability.

Boards may cycle and even regress through various development phases.

Orientation

Orientation occurs when one or more board members that are new join an existing board. Some would characterize the orientation phase as the "honeymoon." Board members, particularly new ones, are excited but cautious, given the new changes. Members should enjoy it while they can because it rarely lasts.

New board members usually lack the proficiency of experienced board members and arrive with no substantial relationships to other board members. The presiding officer should treat these new members with a directive leadership style. This style requires specific procedural directions and real explanations as board proceedings unfold. This direction should only come from the presiding officer or another venerable board member. Other board members should be tolerant of the new leadership style, recognizing it only lasts until new members reach functional competence.

Constructive Conflict

The good feelings and optimism of the orientation phase recede quickly as the reality of opposing positions, conflicting priorities, different viewpoints and pressing matters set in.

For the new members, their agenda and mandate collide with the limitations of governmental regulations, funding restrictions, and limited staff resources. The movement to conflict phase should be viewed as a positive development since the board is evolving constructively toward productivity.

Stresses interpersonal relations among board members occur when newer members, feeling the pressing need to make a change, become dissatisfied. They tend to blame other board members for their frustration. This frustration leads to power struggles over control and the relative importance of individual opinions.

The presiding officer should assume the role of mediator, conducting the meeting as though it were a negotiation ses-

sion among opposing parties. Mediators clarify the conflicting positions, propose compromise solutions and lobby parties to accept the compromise. The objective should be to construct solutions that all members can support, although this goal may not always be possible. The balance of the board should actively resist agreeing to outlandish demands to placate new board members under the mistaken assumption it will improve the board rapport. The board member engagement cycle found under the North: Partnership: Peer Board Members section is an excellent model to follow.

Open Warfare

Particularly strong-willed or dysfunctional board members together with a weak performance by the presiding officer are a sure way to descend from conflict into open warfare. Similar to its military counterpart, board warfare creates casualties with permanent wounds. Grudges, strong dislike, disrespect, distrust and seething revulsion toward another are all probable outcomes that will forever poison the board's rapport and color future decisions. This disunity is a war of will, and anybody who lacks stamina will merely withdraw until the shooting stops. A committee that languishes in warfare will never be productive or proficient until personnel or personal changes occur.

Recognize that in this phase decorum, courtesy and respect are nonexistent. A hostile environment demands a leadership style tantamount to referee or barroom bouncer.

Without question, the strength and will of the presiding officer will determine how long hostilities persist. The presiding officer must be ready to intervene anytime and shut down an acrimonious argument. Action on misconduct must occur immediately and the perpetrator reprimanded or even censured for the most egregious acts. In the very worst cases, a permissive or weak presiding officer may want to hand the gavel over to a more assertive and experienced board member or even appoint an independent facilitator to manage the board meetings under progress begins to occur. Invite the media to attend meetings and the local cable access channel to broadcast board meetings; these actions will have a sobering effect on board member conduct.

Resolution

The resolution phase quickly and usually would follow the constructive conflict phase. Coming out of conflict, board members will have a better understanding of each other, acceptance of uncontrollable limitations, and a higher level of knowledge will exist. The board members will stop seeing each other as the problem. This recognition is excellent preparation for the processes of resolution.

In the resolution, the emphasis moves toward reaching solutions through the give and take of joint problem-solving.

Board members have become more proficient, and relationships are strengthening. The presiding officer should act in the role of facilitator, working with less detailed instructions and providing positive reinforcement. A facilitator leadership style encourages full participation by all board members, complete communication, open-ended questions and a gentle direction toward action. The board should acknowledge the resolved issue and celebrate it as a significant accomplishment that reinforces the solidification of working relationships.

Cooperation

In the cooperation phase, the group becomes mostly self-managed. Most disputes have been resolved. The whole board addresses each issue with a renewed commitment to joint problem-solving. Board members have achieved a level of proficiency, and they feel good about working with each other in a mutually supportive environment. There are high morale and the sense of satisfaction that comes from shared accomplishments.

At this stage, the board members are fully proficient, and working relationships are well established. The appropriate

40

leadership style is passive but with high levels of relationship behavior reinforcing individual contributions and positive outcomes. The role of the presiding officer is to monitor discussion and move board actions along.

Board Members Behaving Badly

From time to time, the election of one or more candidates who are extreme individualists severely affects a board. These types slip into public office as a direct result of public apathy and anger toward all levels of government. Far too many of these types are single-issue candidates, revenge seekers, and self-righteous reformers. Almost all harbor strong negative feelings toward authority figures. Their presence poisons the governance process and reinforces the public stereotype that all public officials are intellectually dishonest and incompetent.

> Single–issue candidates, revenge seekers and self-righteous reformers

Check out this list of real-life antics and misdeeds by dysfunctional board members:

- ▶ Communicate surreptitiously with disgruntled employees to increase their level of dissatisfaction
- ▶ Undermine board decisions by publicly rejecting the decision
- ▶ Attack staff for previous board actions that occurred before one was elected to the board
- ▶ Impeach another, then deny that person the right to a defense

▶ Use theatrics and unrealistic predictions of gloom and doom to sway others

▶ Make available to opponents of the agency, confidential information from closed sessions

▶ Remind agency employees they are overpaid, underworked and incapable of holding a job in private business

▶ Don't participate in board discussion on an issue, then vote no

▶ Blindside management in public with outrageous and insulting accusations

▶ Encourage employees to bypass management and come directly to a board member with their complaints

▶ Judge past actions by today's standards and knowledge

▶ Release confidential documents to agency critics and political candidates

▶ Accuse management of making a particular recommendation because of their political party affiliation or personal political philosophy

▶ Use the official title of board member and the name of the agency to sign the opposing ballot argument to a statewide measure previously endorsed by a full board vote

▶ Micromanage an issue, then blame failure on others

▶ Use aggressive tactics to coerce board members into agreement

▶ Criticize, but offer no realistic solutions

▶ Interrupt and shut down any staff member who disagrees

- ► Always attack the fundamental legitimacy of the agency
- ► Make an unprovoked, vicious personal attack against another, then say "don't take it personally."
- ► Frequently abstain from a vote without explanation
- ► Withhold insider information that would prevent a board error and then later say, "I told you so."
- ► Criticize management in public and in front of employees
- ► Accuse the CEO of stealing personal documents
- ► Challenge management's competence by quoting as an authority an employee who failed an on-the-job random drug test
- ► Adopt an employee and act as their protector at meetings
- ► If the CEO owes up to an honest mistake, remind the CEO at every opportunity
- ► After reviewing the CEO's expense account in a public meeting, intimate that the CEO should be imprisoned
- ► Invite employees to anonymously criticize management and then read their comments aloud at a public meeting
- ► Recruit employees to act as secretive moles and spies

What is impressive about this list is that just a few people exhibited all these deviant behaviors.

One objective: destroy other people and the agency.

What these few have in common is that they are all self-employed, political ideologues, members of fringe political groups and as a result, reject all forms of authority.

Also, note that most of these behaviors have one objective in common: the destruction of other people and the agency. The sad fact is that extreme individualists are hell-bent on destroying government at all levels with their dubious ends justifying their aberrant means. Moreover, to the dismay of many, they are now all too common in local government.

Dealing with Dysfunctional Board Members

Should the board be so unfortunate as to become afflicted with one of these types, proceed cautiously. First, the board should attempt to use all the available skills and techniques outlined in this book to build a collaborative relationship. If this is unsuccessful, one must employ other strategies.

Preserve whatever fragments of relationship one can by continuing to act unconditionally constructive, doing what is good for the agency, irrespective of their response. As hard as it may seem, accept them as they are. Recognize they are not likely to change, nor are they likely to make any positive contribution. Attempt to help them, but only to a certain point, even though they may attack. Expect ingratitude for any act of kindness.

Do not give these persons more credibility than they deserve by spending any significant amount of board time trying to placate them. Grow several layers of thick skin to ward off the insults and derogatory statements they will hurl at you. Develop the spinal strength to stand up to their outrageous demands, fiery rhetoric and long-winded bluster. Carefully consider comments and actions toward them, as they will twist these into rationalizations for their own aggressive misconduct. Be wary of their motives as they are usually hidden and devious. Forget about using logic and reason since they are rigid ideologues who have no interest in hearing information that contradicts their deeply held belief system. Accept the fact that they will never be team players and will always oppose anything that is not their idea. For acts of gross misconduct, the presiding officer and the balance of the board should not shy away from censure.

If one values their sanity, immediately recruit an opposing candidate.

These types can be maddening — precisely what they are trying to achieve. If one values their sanity, immediately start recruiting candidates to run against them in the next election.

Helpful Information

The 3-5 Rule

Throughout this book, one reads, they will notice that points and suggested strategies fall within the Golden Range of 3-5. Three points make a case, more than five overstate. Less than three tasks, suggests one is not doing enough. More than five are overwhelming. Keep this principle in mind when implementing the suggestions in this book. This guide is a good rule of thumb to apply when one is setting a personal agenda, selecting goals or preparing to make a brief public talk.

The Policy v. Administration Conundrum

The policy v. administration question has no black and white answers. Policy and administration are merely opposite ends of a single spectrum where one definition gradually evolves or devolves into the other. Most of the range lies in the middle where there are no clear-cut answers. No wonder the policy-administration conundrum is a never-ending struggle among board members and between the board and management on this subject.

Policy and administration are simply opposite ends of a spectrum.

Just for the record, policy is a broad statement intended to influence and determine governmental decisions and actions. Administration is the execution of decisions and tasks necessary to implement policy. In other words, policy is anything that is not administration and *vice versa*!

Because of the ambiguous nature of most governmental actions, they usually contain elements of both policy and administration. Perhaps the best one can do is paraphrase a Supreme Court justice frustrated at trying to define another ambiguous subject, "I know policy when I see it." The best approach then merely takes a situational approach by letting the facts and circumstances dictate. However, at that time make clear to all that it is mostly one or the other. The following table provides some useful criteria to help classify an action.

	Policy	Administration
Who	Board of Directors	Chief Executive
What	Results	Methods
When	Deadline	Pace
Where	Board Meeting	Field and Office
How	Group Action	Individual Decision

Much of the policy-administration struggle can be resolved by stipulating in a written delegation agreement the specific boundaries for each. The following table provides some comparative examples to help further clarify the issues.

Subject Area	Policy	Administration
Water Use	Water ordinance	Plan review, permits, inspection
Vehicles	Budget allocation	Make, model
Personnel	Budget allocation, personnel policy manual	Recruitment, interview, hiring, salary, termination
Capital Improvements	Budget, schedule, bid award	Design, bidding, construction management
Public Outreach	Budget, plan	Newsletter, tours, event organization

For any board member who is serious about sticking to the policy arena and leaving the details to others, the following template should help formulate policy initiatives.

> I make the motion to direct the (chief executive officer) to (desired results) by (deadline) using (resource allocation) and executed within (reference guideline).

Example:

> I make the motion to direct the <u>General Manager</u> to <u>prepare a district travel and expense policy for board approval</u> by <u>July 1</u>, using <u>existing staff</u> and executed with <u>regard to the Public Trust and prudent business practices.</u>

Big Picture Questions

Getting a handle on the Big Picture is not easy. Most people must discipline themselves to think on this level. Details are easy to understand and grasp. Envisioning the Big Picture requires hard thinking, and most people try to avoid it. To help those who are interested in seeing the Big Picture, here are 10 key questions to think about or pose at a board workshop.

1. **Mission** – Does the agency mission accurately reflect what it does? Does the purpose need to be modified, expanded or reduced?
2. **Form** – Is the form of our agency appropriate for our mission?
3. **Workforce** –Is the workforce adequate in size and competence for our mission? Is there learning and improvement in knowledge, skills, and abilities?

4. **Structure** – Does the internal structure adequately meet the needs of the agency and our mission?

5. **Leadership** – Is there a shared vision and a shared sense of purpose? Do the board and management share common goals and objectives?

6. **Infrastructure** – Is the infrastructure adequate, well maintained and current?

7. **Technology** – Is there widespread use of modern technology? Can the workforce be trained to make full use of technological advancements?

8. **Fiscal** – Is the agency financially secure? How well are funds handled and managed?

9. **Community** – Is the agency responsive to community needs? Does the community hold the agency accountable for its actions?

10. **Effectiveness** – How well does the agency do its job? Is it the most cost-effective approach?

Current Issues Workshop

Strategic planning may be a fun exercise, but strategic planning does little to answer the burning issues of the here and now. It is this "in your face" issues that trouble many agencies. Nagging, unresolved matters play heavy on board relationships and can become a source of irritation if allowed to fester too long. They can infiltrate their way into otherwise unrelated routine actions, creating delay and frustration. One solution is to set aside time away from the stress of the regular board meeting. At this meeting, carefully focus on pressing questions and challenges. In other words, conduct a current issues workshop.

Begin by establishing a date and time commitment for each board member and the chief executive. Select a location within the agency boundaries but away from agency offices.

Solicit agenda topics for the workshop from each board member and the chief executive. The presiding officer or a committee appointed by the presiding officer should work with the chief executive to consolidate, prioritize and caption each issue. Limit the agenda to only these issues and follow the 3-5 Rule.

Select an independent facilitator to run the meeting using the appropriate group process technique. Using a facilitator levels the playing field relieves the presiding officer of the burden of running the meeting and allows for full participation by all board members. A facilitator is efficient and provides a neutral party to control the debate. If some board members balk at the cost, just add up the time value of all participants and assume a facilitator will cut down the workshop time by at least half. Let the facilitator use his/her group process skills to move the group toward consensus and resolution.

A facilitator can save as much as 50% of board time.

Other members of the management team may attend, but should largely remain as observers or as an on-call knowledgeable resource. Limit the number of active participants since more voices reduce valuable dialogue time among board members.

Have the facilitator summarize the workshop outcome. Place this summary on a future agenda for review and possible action. Keep in mind just giving an individual an opportunity to have his/her say quells many problems. Circulate the results of the workshop among staff and the community. Repeat the workshop process annually or more frequently, if appropriate.

References and Further Reading

1. *Power to Persuade* by Richard Haas
2. *Getting to Yes* by Roger Fisher and William Ury
3. *Getting Past No* by William Ury
4. *Leaders* by Warren Bennis
5. *Getting It Done* by Roger Fisher and Alan Sharp
6. *Art of War* by Sun Tzu
7. *Situational Leader* by Paul Hersey
8. *High Performance Teams* by Ken Blanchard and others
9. *Boards that Make a Difference* by John Carver
10. *Beyond Machiavelli* by Roger Fisher and others
11. *The Third Side* by William Ury

Practical Politics Template

If a reader has purchased this book, he/she has limited permission to duplicate the template on the next page for personal use. Make an 8 ½ x 11 copy in landscape orientation with the compass face in the center. Using the compass points metaphor in this book, place the appropriate political landmarks at each cardinal point. Consider the navigation techniques listed by each cardinal point. Refer to the "Chart the Course" section for more information. Use the finished map to navigate to greater political success!

INFLUENCE
SOVEREIGNTY
PARTNERSHIP
AUTHORITY
Understanding
Persuasion
Communication
Trustworthiness
Reason & Logic
Acceptance
Public View
Visibility
Respectful
Shape Opinion
Big Picture
Board
Agenda
Competence
Trust
Public View
Expectations
Evaluation
Advisor
Policy Only
Relationship
Whole Board
Engage All
Consensus

About the Author

David C. Antonucci is a civil and environmental engineering graduate of California Polytechnic State University and Oregon State University. He has enjoyed a 41-year public career, including 20 years as general manager and chief engineer of a multifunction special district in the Lake Tahoe area. He retired in 2000 at age 49. During his tenure, his district received over 50 awards of recognition for excellence in water, sewer and parks and recreation services. Moreover, the agency was consistently the most cost-effective service provider among similar agencies in the region, while having the highest level of service standards. He has worked with and served on numerous public agency and non-profit boards as a public official and private citizen.

The author is Principal Consultant for Management Support Professionals, a management consulting firm serving local government. He specializes in facilitation and group process; workshops and training; organizational troubleshooting; and interim management assignments. Management Support Professionals offers value priced fees and condensed services that are affordable for smaller entities. For further information, you may contact Management Support Professional at 530-525-5410 or by email at dcantonucci@msn.com.

www.ingramcontent.com/pod-product-compliance
Lightning Source LLC
Chambersburg PA
CBHW061524250726
48657CB00005B/2069